CW01305730

Spiritual Concepts

The Simple Truth

A Beginners Guide to a Spiritual Journey.

Carol Anne Stacey

authorHOUSE®

AuthorHouse™ UK Ltd.
500 Avebury Boulevard
Central Milton Keynes, MK9 2BE
www.authorhouse.co.uk
Phone: 08001974150

© 2009 Carol Anne Stacey. All rights reserved.

No part of this book may be reproduced, stored in a retrieval system, or transmitted by any means without the written permission of the author.

First published by AuthorHouse 5/4/2009

ISBN: 978-1-4389-5977-1 (sc)

Printed in the United States of America
Bloomington, Indiana

This book is printed on acid-free paper.

A Beginners Guide to a Spiritual Journey

This is a book of the basic understanding of our spiritual connections. I am trying to give simple answers to many questions that have been asked by my clients and students.

It is about our fears, frustrations and insecurities that surround us every day, and the answer to the question 'Do Angels and Guides really hear me when I speak to them'?

I will give the simple truth, as I see it, and I will try to show every reader how to trust and never give up on your connection to the world of spirit. I shall explain the tests we go through and the reasons why, and will try to answer truthfully and honestly. Remember, my truths are not necessarily your truths, but I do hope to open your heart to find what you have been searching for. Those answers can be found within your own heart, I will show you how to retrieve them.

Enjoy the journey.

Dedication.

This book is dedicated to all the people who have and do believe in me. To all the clients and students, who have put their trust in my ability to help them have a better quality of life.

We have shared dreams and shed tears together, but most of all we have built a bond of love and trust. I thank you from the bottom of my heart.

I write this book for all who follow on, searching for their spiritual connection.

If I can offer any advice it would be to always trust the 'Higher Beings' of Light who will be there for you in every way. They will never let you down, that I promise.

I have been shown so much Love and trust from the 'Hierarchy' this gives me the confidence to move forward with my mission here on Earth. Bringing healing to humanity, helping them to open their hearts and therefore allowing them to have a change in consciousness.

My Guardian Angel Thomas, my Rahanni guide Kira, all of the Archangels, Angels,

Melchizedek and Kwan Yin. I humbly thank you for your channelling and teachings that have helped me to create this second book.

With deepest gratitude I thank you all.

Acknowledgements.

I wish to thank AuthorHouse for all their help and assistance in the production of this book.

They give every writer a wonderful opportunity to express their beliefs, where in the literary world today there is so much prejudice and snobbery. It is refreshing to find a company willing to give many of us who are not as academic as they possibly need to be but who still have a message to get out to the masses.

Without companies such as AuthorHouse our voices would not be heard. I thank you once again on behalf of all the writers that you have helped in publishing their work.

I also wish to thank the White Eagle Publishing Trust for their kind permission allowing me to use quotations from the wonderful teachings of White Eagle.

Introduction.

This is a book for all beginners on a spiritual journey and their need for questions to be answered honestly and simply. – No complications.

I believe and know that everyone on this planet has the seed-atom or connection to Source/God. Otherwise we wouldn't be here.

Many people are searching and are ready to have more understanding of spiritual consciousness; others haven't arrived at that time in their earthly life to take these spiritual concepts on board. It is called Divine Timing, what is right for one person is not necessarily right for another. No judgement is made.

For those of you who are ready, you will no doubt be searching for the books to give you the right information. There are so many out there and it can get very confusing. All you want is the basic understanding, nothing too heavy or scientific. This is where I come in. I am offering the reader the simple truths of spirituality. No clever words, no scientific jargon, just the basic facts. You will be presented with just enough information to awaken your desire for more in-depth information at the appropriate time.

So, here it is. I do hope, as you read through, something will touch you deep inside helping you to feel comfortable and ready to search for your inner truth.

The purpose of your life is to develop the understanding and power of your own spiritual uniqueness and essence.

When you arrived into this incarnation you were not alone, you brought with you your own special Guardian Angel and guides to help you on your journey of discovery.

You can get to know your guides through meditation; this will help to raise your consciousness to a higher level of spiritual understanding. This, and many other ways of connecting, will be offered to you within the teachings of this book. Bringing forward the spiritual knowledge that your soul is already aware of; I will show you a way of retrieving this wisdom, which you have held within your being for eons of time.

Join me now on a wonderful journey of discovery of the simple truths and the essence of your being. Recognising your connection to Source/God and all 'Higher Beings' of Light and Love.

Contents

CHAPTER ONE
Are you there? 1

CHAPTER TWO
Growing Again 10

CHAPTER 3
Holding on to Inner Strength. 15

CHAPTER FOUR
Connecting to Guides and Angels 20

CHAPTER FIVE
Much is given but much is expected. 25

CHAPTER SIX
Expanding your consciousness. 29

CHAPTER SEVEN
Ascension, what does this mean? 32

CHAPTER EIGHT
Reincarnation – Does it really happen? 34

CHAPTER NINE
Karma – Law of Cause and Effect 39

Chapter Ten

Meditation – Why is it important? 42

Chapter Eleven

What is the 'Age of Aquarius'? 46

Chapter Twelve

Understanding Soul Mates. 49

Chapter Thirteen

What happens when we die? 53

Chapter Fourteen

How to get the best out of life. 59

Chapter Fifteen

A simple approach to life. 63

Chapter Sixteen

Between two worlds. 71

Chapter Seventeen

Healing Hands. 77

Chapter One
Are you there?

Many people ask me, 'Do Guides, Angels and Ascended Masters really communicate with us and if they do why can't we all hear them'? There are many reasons why you don't hear, and one in particular is that you do not trust what is being presented to you. You dismiss the connection by saying, 'Oh, that is just my imagination.' So you bring in doubt.

Let me share with you something that happened to me not that long ago, infact it was on the 26th August 2007 at 9.30p.m. I began a meditation, as this is my quiet time in the evening. I am a healer and teacher of spiritual concepts and most evenings I will be sending distant healing to many sick people. Some I know, some I don't, but that is of no consequence as no judgement is made at any time.

I know that healing has been received by the telephone calls I get from grateful families.

This particular evening was significant in the fact that during the day I had an overwhelming feeling or sense of being alone. I felt sad, but didn't know why, but it was the loneliness that hit me and I felt very tearful.

Now this may sound crazy because I am never alone, my husband Barrie has been with me through thick and thin over 44 years and is very supportive of my spiritual understanding. I have 4 beautiful daughters who contact me on a regular basis, and I have clients and students that are always popping in and out of my home daily. So why should I feel desperately lonely? I didn't have an answer; all I knew was the feeling inside was a feeling of abandonment and sadness. Why?

As I sat in the chair in my healing room, rushing through my mind was question after question. 'Do my guides really hear me, do angels actually communicate with me and do Ascended Masters actually channel information through me? So the questions went on. This didn't make sense, here I am, a teacher of spiritual and Angel workshops, and all of a sudden I have doubts and I am asking the questions that students would ask me. What was going on?

I began to relax and thought to myself – right, let's start at the beginning, I will think like a novice as though I have never communicated with guides or written anything before. As a novice I need answers to basic questions. So I called out; 'Angels, guides and any Higher Being of Light, do you hear anything I ask and more important are you really there?' I waited, it was as though I had gone back to my teenage years, not really understanding the spiritual side of life. Always believed in Jesus and I didn't really know why at that time, but it was something very strong inside of me that felt so right. When I looked at pictures depicting Jesus I always felt a warmth and a love; the eyes would say so much; but I digress.

So here I am still waiting for an answer, I sat quietly and thinking; 'Is there a God out there in the universe with Ascended Masters and Archangels?' Suddenly I heard this voice inside my head say – 'One question at a time.' I didn't respond straight away, so it was repeated. 'One question at a time.' I began to look around my room, I couldn't see anything, but I was feeling very warm and tingly. I asked. 'Are you really communicating with me or is this my imagination working overtime?'

I listened for the reply, straight away I heard; 'You may call it imagination but this is a word that is difficult to explain. Yes I am communicating with you through your imagination because that part of your brain is so very close to Source/God. It has a light beaming from your physical brain that radiates out towards higher dimensions of reality.

Every human on your planet has imagination, this is a gift presented to you when you incarnate on to this earth plane. When you raise your vibration spiritually this expands and helps us – guides, angels and all 'Higher Beings' of Light connect and communicate with you. When you become aware of how this works you will accept this very easily, it will become second nature to you and you will be strengthening the connection without forcing it.' I listened intently but wanted to know to whom I was speaking. Before I could ask, I heard, 'My name is Thomas, I am your Guardian Angel, and yes, we have telepathy.' Thomas, oh how brilliant, a name I can call in times of need.

Again he interrupted my thoughts, 'In the higher dimensions we do not have names, as we are known by the Light that emanates from our being, the vibration surrounding us, this will change of course as we progress, but let us continue to keep this simple, after all, isn't this what your book is about, simple truths?' This made me smile; he is one step ahead of me.

Thomas continued to give more information. 'Every human also has a personality and this is how we send the information required. How we explain to one person on the earth will be different to how we explain to another. The reason is we have to connect to the level of spiritual understanding that you have reached in this incarnation. If someone is at a scientific level we will tap into that personality and deliver information scientifically. I couldn't do that with you, no judgement is meant, we try to make it easier for you, do you understand?' Yes, I understood perfectly. Thomas continued. 'So the way we show a person how to express spiritual concepts is not necessarily the way we would show another. We, the spiritual hierarchy, know instantly how to communicate with you, through your personalities. I wish to explain imagination to you so you can share this information with your students.

'You have a wonderful Teacher on the Earth known as White Eagle, he has a beautiful way of explaining imagination, I shall use his words as they are a simple truth which I am sure you will appreciate.'

'Don't be afraid of your imagination. Many of you fear that the vivid thoughts you have are possibly an over-active imagination. This is not so, you dismiss a lot of precious moments that have happened to you by saying; Oh that couldn't have happened, it's all in my mind. Your lower earthly mind is destroying the realisation of a beautiful event that happened in a previous life. Don't forget we have about 200 incarnations and our soul knows of every event and all that has happened in these lifetimes.

We have a celestial body that stores all past life memories. Sometimes our soul can retrieve them and they are brought forward into our conscious mind, or our imagination.

Whenever you see pictures in your imagination you are seeing spiritual clairvoyance.

All that has been before is already held within your soul. If it were not and hadn't happened you could not bring it forward to create the picture you see in your mind or imagination. So please remember, do not doubt what you are given to see. These are your truths; always know that in your heart. Even if your imagination conjures up pictures of death and destruction, this is also your truth.

Because you have had many incarnations don't think they were all wonderful and beautiful; nothing would be gained or learned if they were. It's all about balance, you have lived positive happy existences, but you have also lived through pain and suffering. Your soul knows your truth. Learn to trust your imagination a little more.'

This was all beginning to make sense. I knew in my heart that I was communicating with 'Higher Beings' of Light, but we as humans always mistrust what is being presented to us as fanciful imagination.

My inner truths began to awaken once more as Thomas continued with the information. Everything seemed so right again, I felt connected. I was happy that I was back to the real me again. I wanted more information to pass on to my students - would he be happy to answer more questions? 'Yes' he replied, but remember, your truths are not necessarily anyone else's truths, make sure you explain this to your students.'

One of the questions I needed answering was important to me personally, so I asked Thomas, 'Why in the past few days was my spiritual connection taken from me, I know it was only for a short time but I felt so sad and alone?' Thomas replied in a loving way. 'This had to happen dear one so you could understand how others feel without their connection to the truth of who they really are. As a teacher of spiritual concepts this was an important lesson for you, and I am happy that coming back to your spiritual self makes you feel whole again. I do hope you can understand.' I certainly did, but I must say it has helped me to become stronger and appreciative of my connections to the higher realms. I will never take any of this for granted. It brings me joy every day of my life and I still feel very humble with regards to the spiritual gifts and trust that has been given to me.

All I can do is give people my understanding, this will of course help others come to their own conclusion, and it does give them food for thought.

Thomas continued to offer more insight into the ways of spirit; he gave me some information that I wish to share with you that I feel is quite important.

'Many people on the earth plane know of Mother Teresa of Calcutta whose wonderful work with children was a joy to behold, but understand this; there were many times in her life when dealing with so much pain and suffering that Mother Teresa would say,' 'I have searched all my life for acceptance of God and at times didn't feel or see anything with regards to spirit, but I **_knew._**' Thomas continued to explain. 'Do you see, it was a feeling deep inside her heart that trusted, it was a knowing, something you cannot quantify or explain but it was felt in the heart centre, the centre of our being. Everyone on this planet will have that feeling sometime in their existence. It is the spark, the connection to Source/God. One day you will all recognise this and will know the truth of your being.'

Thomas continued by saying, 'Let me ask you a question, what do you think is the purpose of life? Speak from your heart but take your time.'

Wow! I wasn't expecting to be questioned, but it was relevant as I am a teacher of spiritual concepts. I took a deep breath and replied. 'My first reaction would be to say having my children, giving them values, showing them how to be kind and compassionate, but I know deep inside of my being that it is more than that. I am here to grow spiritually to work with love and compassion, to release negative thoughts and fear based thinking and to be accepting in my heart that I am a Divine spark of Light going through many interesting experiences, some happy others sad; but they will all help to make me the person I aim to be. A person of love and Light bringing hope, and healing to my fellow man.'

I hoped this answer was acceptable to Thomas. I felt his energy move closer to mine as he spoke. 'Very well understood, but it is also more than that. Every one of you has a special mission, to develop your character/personality, and this will only happen as you go through your experiences, but much more important is that you serve Source/God and humanity, helping them to understand their own Divinity and their connection to Source. The truth of your existence lies within yourself and at the appropriate time this will be shown to you.' I thanked Thomas for that information, as I knew it to be true.

I also knew that if I have felt out of kilter or a bit low, or have moved away and questioned my spiritual side, I know how alone I feel, how insignificant and miserable I become. But as soon as I have my connection once again I feel alive, happy and full of optimism for the future.

I have dealt with many difficult and painful experiences in this life, [See my first book Rahanni Celestial Healing – Embracing the Light] and I know deep inside how much I have learned from them. I am a great believer that we do not make mistakes, we go through experiences.

It was getting quite late and I was feeling tired, Thomas felt this and he suggested we bring this evening to a close, continuing when I had rested. He bade me farewell as his energies gently moved away.

US AS
SOUL EXTENSIONS/PERSONALITIES

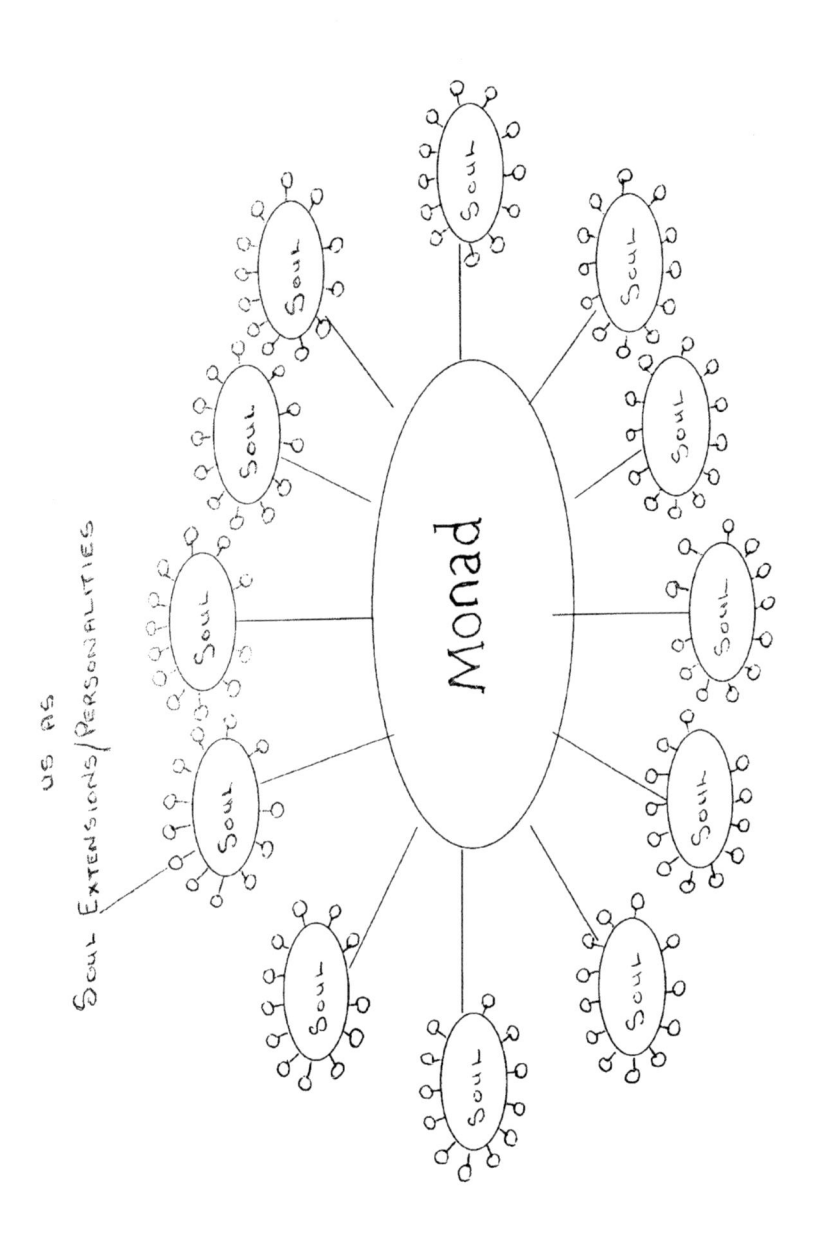

CHAPTER TWO
Growing Again

Let me return to the beginning, the first spark of Light, our natural essence.

First we are a soul in a physical body going through life's experiences helping us to grow and climb our spiritual ladder. I will give you the interpretation of the journey of the soul. I have enclosed a diagram opposite; I hope you find it easy to follow.

This information has been taken from the book 'The Complete Ascension Manual' by Dr. Joshua David Stone.

The Monad is a Divine spark from Source/God. [See chart.] It is also known as the 'I am Presence' It was the first core intelligence and individualised identity. It also had freedom of choice. This intelligence decided it wanted to experience a denser form of the material universe than it was living in. So each of our monads with the power of its mind created 12 souls. Each soul is a smaller and partial representation of its creator the monad. The soul is also known as the higher self, the super-conscious mind and higher mind.

So Source/God created millions of monads and each monad created 12 individualised souls. Each soul then deciding to experience a denser form of the material universe created 12 soul extensions or personalities and that is us. So we on Earth are personalities or soul extensions of our soul, just as our soul is an extension of a greater consciousness, our monad. Our monad is an even greater consciousness of Source/God, the Godhead, the Mother and Father of all creation.

Each of us on Earth has a soul family so to speak; we have 11 other soul extensions. Some could be incarnated on Earth at this time, some on another planet within the infinite universe. Each of us has 12 in our soul group and 144 in our monadic group.

An Ascended Master named Djwhal Khul [pronounced Dwall Kool.] has stated that there are 60 thousand million monads working through our earthly planetary system. So if we multiply 60 thousand million by 144 we have the number of soul extensions or personalities involved in the process of reincarnation on this planet.

Are you still with me? Don't worry too much about this information, all will become clear when you raise your vibration just that little bit more. It is something you can refer back to at a later date.

Going back to my first chapter, I had at some point lost my connection to my spiritual side. [For a very good reason that has been explained.] I wasn't happy and felt utterly miserable, but as I have often said we have to experience the negative to appreciate the positive. This brings me to a part in my life and understanding that maybe you have felt at sometime but didn't want to recognise what was happening.

All the years I have been married, [44 to be precise] from quite early on I was the one that had to make sure that everything was running smoothly and that Barrie, my husband, was happy. I was a giver by nature, don't get me wrong – I was happy to give, I always felt comfortable in that role. The difficulty I had was receiving, this felt alien to me, it wasn't natural. This was how things were in the 50s and 60s, the woman's place was in the home looking after her man and the man provided. So Victorian, but most of us knew no different.

I continued for many years doing what Barrie wanted. If he didn't feel like going out with friends we didn't go, if he wasn't in the mood for talking, we didn't talk. Every day was built around his wants and needs, not once did I question or ask myself what did I want to do. I just carried on, give, give, give. I couldn't have a conversation with him because he was always right – so he said. If I tried to say something to get my point across and he didn't like what I had said, he would go quiet or not speak to me for hours. He would sulk, like most men at that time they had to have their own way.

He had been thoroughly spoiled as a child and still expected the same from me. Now this sounds terrible, as though I am living with a monster; that isn't so. All I am trying to get across is how easy it is for people like us to carry on in the same old way for a quiet life. In the end we lose our own identity, we don't know who we really are. We are so concerned in keeping others happy that we forget ourselves, our needs.

Looking back I recognised Barrie's behaviour was the example set by his parents, not that they were nasty, in fact they were lovely people but with Victorian ideas.

There have been occasions when people ask me why I stayed with someone so angry and negative. My answer is that I know Barrie has a heart, I have seen it when he feeds the Robin by hand in the garden, with temperatures below freezing and he has emphysema, [chronic lung disease.] I remember the time I had to go to hospital to have an endoscopy [camera down the throat] ugh! Not a pleasant experience, but because of this procedure I wasn't allowed any food for hours. I asked Barrie what he wanted for breakfast and he said he didn't feel like eating, he wasn't hungry. Now that is not Barrie, he has a very big appetite, but it turns out, he realised I couldn't eat so he didn't think it was fair that he ate in front of me, so he waited until I had gone to the hospital. That is a man with a heart.

I am giving you a close up of my personal experiences because I want you to know that as you become stronger spiritually you will change. I most certainly have. You wake up one day – literally and say to yourself, that's it, I am worth more than this, and I will not be dictated to again. I have needs just as anyone else and I will start to put myself first for a change and learn to say no. I am not saying it was easy, but because of the inner strength I found due to my spiritual connection, I control my life, not Barrie or anyone else.

I do understand why he and I stayed together. He is my soul mate and in a sense he has been my teacher as I have been his. We have a different relationship now, which has made for a happier marriage.

It has taken many years and many traumas to find

my inner strength and to get me to where I am now. I am still learning and will continue to do so as this is what life is about.

CHAPTER 3
Holding on to Inner Strength.

I am now 65 years of age and I have grown in leaps and bounds especially within the past 6 years. It possibly seems quite late in life for me to have all these changes happening and new directions, but I say it's never too late for positive change. Don't forget your guide and soul know when the time is right for you to move forward and progress; it's called 'Divine Timing.'

Always remember, nothing is wasted, it is a gift from Source/God. We are presented with certain situations in our life at the time when we will receive the best possible opportunities for our spiritual growth. So it is of no consequence what age we are presented with these Golden experiences, it is how we deal with each one. Some may be happy and some difficult and sad. Welcome, to the school of spiritual learning. The most difficult of all our journeys will be here on this Earth. But believe me, many souls are queuing up to continue their education at a very high level, here on this earth plane.

Many of us on a spiritual path have cleared 51% of our karma. [Karma – The law of cause and effect. What you give out you will get back.] We all have Karma to deal with. This is something you can't get away from.

I am no different to anyone else, just because I am a channel for healing and a spiritual teacher doesn't mean I am perfectly balanced. I am still learning and I will always be the student while I am here on this Earth.

It is a joy to know that I have progressed in a very short space of time. Gone is the weak woman with no confidence or self esteem, to a woman who knows where she is and where she comes from. I have found an inner strength, but most of all I care for me, I am able to say I love myself. For when I am loving myself, I am loving Source/God, as I believe we are all a part of the whole, the great universal Light. There is no separation.

Having this trust and these feelings brings so much joy into my life. I feel the compassion for everything, for my family, friends, everything in nature, birds, animals, trees, rivers, mountains, flowers, crystals and the beautiful Earth. Not forgetting the wonderful Ascended Masters, Archangels, Angels and all Higher Beings of Light. The joy in my heart is forever there, no one can take that from me. I am in control, I feel and I know.

I thank the universe Source/God for my experiences in this lifetime, because it has awakened me to who I truly am. A Light Worker who decided thousands of years ago to be here at this moment in time to serve Source/God and humanity, helping to heal children and adults in whatever way I could with love and compassion. I will hold on to that inner strength and will stay true to myself and I will continue to teach by example.

Many of you will want to know how to get the inner strength in the first place, especially if your journey here so far has been nothing but doom and gloom. I am not saying it is easy, but anything that is worthwhile and can change your current situation deserves the time spent on it. You may initially go to a healer or counsellor; someone that you feel can understand your situation. They give you guidance and will be able to show you the first steps to having the life you deserve.

You need to be perfectly honest with yourself and assess your life at this time. Ask many questions and write down the answers truthfully. I would suggest making a list of all the negative things in your life, past and present, then a list of all the positive, past and present.

This is very helpful, as long as you are honest; otherwise you are back to square one.

Go way back into your earliest memories, no matter how painful. All issues that need to be removed from your life can be helped by following this advice.

Take an A4 sheet of paper and write everything down that makes you angry or fearful, put all these feelings on the paper. Clear out all the nasty thoughts, keep writing, even if it's just the odd word, let it flow out. It doesn't have to make sense because **you will not read it back**. This is important. By writing things down you are releasing all stored up dross, fears and negativity, if you read it back you are absorbing again, this defeats the object. So, to recap, you clear your mind by writing down, you **don't read it back**, and then you tear it up and burn it. [In a metal bucket.] This is also very important, because smoke is a cleanser. All the words on the paper are energy that will go out into the ether, when it is burned those words and feelings are gone, never to return; providing you continue with positive thought from now on. I recommend that this is done as many times as you feel the need, then maybe once a month. It really works. It is wonderful to see all your pain and sadness being taken away as the flames release you from the pain you have been holding on to for such a long time. This allows you to take responsibility for your health.

You will be surprised how uplifted you begin to feel, and how much stronger you are mentally and emotionally. Many of my clients use this system of clearing on a regular basis.

In this chapter we are discussing how to hold on to inner strength. Some people feel because they are on a spiritual path now that it is necessary to change the personality and become 'Holier than Thou' this is not so.

All that is required to become a stronger person is having beliefs, values and acknowledging your own uniqueness. But it doesn't mean to say you have to let go of the real you and become such a different person that nobody recognises you. Your personality was given for a reason, this is what makes you an individual, but I am trying to say you can bring together both parts of your being. Your personality combined with love, compassion and kindness. This is the real you, your connection to Source/God. This is where you find your inner strength, deep inside of your being.

You will read many spiritual books that state, you must let go of ego and think in your 'Godley' way. I am sorry, but you are still a human being living on the Earth, and the ego needs to be controlled I agree, but we are talking about releasing the negative ego, this doesn't serve our higher purpose. This is one of the lessons here on Earth and can be quite a tricky one to clear. We will never clear this 100% while we are journeying on life's highway, but you can definitely lose 90% in this incarnation.

Ego is somewhat misinterpreted. Yes, I recognise there's many egotistical people in this world, and some do go over the top and take this part of their personality too far. But ego can give you the confidence you may lack, and you need to be a confident person if you are going to reach out to others with a message of love and spiritual understanding. It helps you to express views without getting bigheaded. Therefore people will listen to your words of wisdom. If you are too meek and mild no one will listen and if there isn't enough conviction in your voice, everything falls by the wayside. So you dig deep and find that inner strength. I know by experience, believe me, and it has been something I have had to work at, it didn't come easy.

Since I have found the real me I try to reach out to people by having more intent in my voice. We need this to get our message out to the world. So, we all need a little bit of ego, not in a 'Look at me' type of ego but a stronger personality full of hope for the future. If you combine this with love, compassion and kindness you will make a difference, but it has to come from deep within your heart.

You will find that inner strength by trusting the many guides and Angels that surround you daily. Helping you to grow, and protecting you from negativity, filling your aura with the love and Light of the universe.

Chapter Four
Connecting to Guides and Angels

When we speak of the Angelic Kingdom many people have a picture in their mind of Angels with wings sitting on a cloud playing a harp. Yes, I suppose that does happen, but there is so much more. Angels are androgynous; this means they are balanced with both masculine and feminine energies. They have never incarnated on Earth as they are of the highest vibration and very close to Source/God. Many are showing more of their feminine side or should I say the qualities of compassion and nurturing, as they help humanity move forward on their spiritual journey. If a message needs to go out to the world with intent it will be accomplished with the stronger masculine side. It is beautifully done.

For the past 2000 years we have lived in the age of a more masculine energy, which was required in one respect helping to bring forward strength and for the creation of technology; progression this is called however, as time has passed the masculine energy has been too dominant and has got out of hand, hence the wars and the power struggles that seem to be taking place on a daily basis. This could not continue without having disastrous results. Universal Law is about balance and from the year 2000 changes have taken place. Many people are now saying, 'there has got to be more to life than this.' As soon as the guides hear this they know it is the correct time to present information concerning your spiritual path.

The 'Age of Aquarius' is upon us; the feminine energy is full of Love, Compassion, Hope and Joy. These qualities are desperately needed at this difficult time in our existence on this Earth. We only have to look at the pain and destruction that is taking place within our society to recognise that this cannot continue without having devastating effects.

Too many closed hearts represented by anger, judgement, hate, jealousy and negative energies, all born out of fear not love. This can change and is changing as humanity opens to their spiritual understanding. Something is beginning to stir inside of people as they ask, 'what can I do, how can I help?' Your guide and your higher consciousness will join together and bring through all the relevant information that is appropriate for your spiritual growth.

Guides, Archangels, Angels and 'Higher Beings' of Light are waiting for your call. Remember, in universal law no guide or Angel can interfere in your life unless you ask. They recognise you have free will and freedom of choice, but as soon as they receive your call for help they will do whatever they can to guide you spiritually. It brings them great joy, for as they step forward to support you they are also growing and progressing. This is their reason for 'being' to serve humanity and Source/God.
All you need is patience, not a virtue for many on this earth plane. But combined with trust you will connect to your individual guide.

You may ask, 'how do I begin?' Let me explain, to be in a relaxed atmosphere is important, especially if this is your first attempt at connecting to the many Angels surrounding us at this challenging time. But saying that, you are able to connect with these wonderful beings any time you feel the need. At work, in your car, it is of no consequence, for these guides and Angels are but a touch away wherever you are.

If you can connect to these 'beings' of Light in the quiet of your own home, this would be much more practical. Take yourself to an area or room that feels comfortable and relaxing, close the door, take the telephone off the hook, and switch off your mobile phone. Have the lights down low and if possible light a candle or two. This all helps to create the appropriate atmosphere, helping your connection. Maybe you would prefer some background music conducive to this occasion; go with the flow, just relax.

You are now in your space, your eyes are closed; gently breathe in and out, not forcing this in any way. Don't worry if mundane thoughts start popping into your mind, just let them pass by. Take your thoughts towards your breathing; this will help relax your shoulders. If you are good at visualising, take yourself to an area in your mind that has lovely memories for you, a walk on a beach, or wooded area, just let it happen. You will find the mundane thoughts leaving as you begin to feel an inner peace. This is the time for you to start your communication to your guide or Angel. Just mentally ask a simple question, maybe you could say, 'my dear guide could you please give me a sign that you can hear me.' Now stay relaxed, don't force anything. The more you are in your quiet space the easier it is for them to connect. At first you might feel a slight touch or tickle on the side of your face, or your hair moving. This is your guide trying to communicate. It is all very subtle and you may think not a lot is happening, but continue to trust, this is important. Don't have too many expectations at first, because the logical left side of your brain will be fighting with the right spiritual side. Both sides will eventually become balanced, but of course this takes time. Practice and trust is the key to opening to your higher self. We dismiss a great deal of information that is presented to us by saying it is all in our imagination. Yes, that is one way your guide will find it easier to communicate with you. This is very important. [Read the chapter on imagination again.]

You will eventually find the best way to contact these 'Higher Beings' of Light. All it takes is practice, patience and trust. There are many books that can help you with channelling information and those I recommend are books and CDs by Lita de Alberdi 'Channelling for Healers' and another by Sanaya Roman 'Opening to Channel' Both are beautifully presented and I have used them on a number of occasions.

You could try to join a group that consists of 4/5 people that get together on a regular basis for meditation and channelling. Or better still set up your own group. When you have group energy this will add to the raising of your vibration. Find someone that has an established centre, this will make it easier for beginners of spiritual growth.

Chapter Five

Much is given but much is expected.

Oh! Don't I know it. I could write a book on the tests I have been through, but for now I will give you some idea of how this happens.

I feel very privileged to be a member of the 'White Eagle Lodge' in Hampshire. His teachings touch my heart like no other. If you get the opportunity to read any of White Eagle books please do, I am sure you will love them. One of White Eagle's sayings is 'keep on keeping on' I have lost count of the amount of times I say this to myself. Every time I am hit by a difficult situation the old me would have been in fear or very negative, but now I say 'keep on keeping on' and I ask White Eagle to help me understand the reason for this latest setback. I meditate and connect to my dear friend, as that is how I feel towards White Eagle. He is a friend to everyone. I have also learned to become relaxed, calm and patient; as I know I will eventually receive my answer. It will either be shown in a dream or in seconds of me asking for clarification. I am given a picture in my 3rd eye centre [our intuitive area.] that shows me the reason for the experience at this time. You must learn to trust what is being offered to you.

I want to share something with you that was quite wonderful. I still feel very humble and amazed at the experience. One evening, feeling rather low, I took to my healing room, lit some candles, put on some relaxing music and began to meditate. I had been feeling very connected to White Eagle of late and wanted to pursue this connection. I mentally asked 'Is there anything that you feel I need to work on with regards to myself, helping me become a stronger person and to help with my spiritual growth?' I continued the meditation and felt a gentle breeze around my face and a very strong presence. There was a pulsing and humming sound that I hadn't heard before.

Suddenly I heard in my head a voice saying, 'open your eyes.' As I did, to my amazement in front of me was a shimmering vibration of Golden Light. It became a form or shape that was indicative of White Eagle. As I gazed upon this beautiful energy, tears streamed down my face. I felt the love flow between us; it was one of those truly spiritual moments; it was magical. This Golden glow remained for about 1 minute; although I was so captivated by the beauty it could possibly have been longer. I will never be able to explain the feeling of pure unconditional love that emanated from White Eagle's aura. It literally took my breath away. That feeling will stay with me forever. But this is not the end of the story. By the time I had finished meditating it must have been 9.30p.m. I eventually went to bed at around 11p.m. still so excited at the wonderful experience. So what did White Eagle want me to focus on, I felt it hadn't been made clear, but I trusted and knew something would be presented to me shortly. Little did I know it would happen the following morning. At 7a.m. the post arrived, a large envelope dropped through the letterbox. As I opened the contents I couldn't believe my eyes, there in my hands was a White Eagle course. Its title was 'How to work with your intuition.'

Now I know I hadn't purchased this from the White Eagle Lodge. There was no covering letter, no payment slip, just the manual. I decided to telephone the 'Lodge' just to check, maybe I had forgotten ordering this course. I spoke to the lady who deals with all purchases, she checked my account and all records but no, there was no trace of me ordering this. I explained to the lady what had happened and she laughed as she said, 'I have heard of White Eagle working in mysterious ways but I have never heard of this happening before.' We both agreed he definitely listened to my request for guidance and has come up with a wonderful way of replying. The lady explained that I could return the course, but I knew in my heart that this is an area that White Eagle wishes me to work on. I of course paid for the item and as I read through I completely understood why I had to have this. It certainly gave me more insight into understanding intuition.

I wanted to share this experience with you because you never know when or how these 'Higher Beings' of Light will make their connection to you.

Be aware – be open to the messages that are being brought forward to every one of us. It may come from Angels, your guides or the Ascended Masters.

It is so beautiful to feel the love that surrounds us daily. Just go within and shut out the every day interruptions that stop us from progressing. Let the Light from Source/God radiate into your soul, your heart and your mind. You will become one – a feeling of joy, inner peace and contentment will fill every space of your being.

So the more I give to my spiritual growth the more beautiful gifts I receive. This will happen to you; of that you can be sure. Your guides will fill your life with the spiritual gifts of the Universe, knowing that with every one offered it will be used in helping humanity to find their individual path to enlightenment.

Chapter Six

Expanding your consciousness.

To receive the spiritual gifts that are offered, you must expand your consciousness. It will take time, but I will share with you ways in which you can create this wondrous experience.

First, let us ask 'what is consciousness?' It is an aspect of 'being', our natural essence shining through, something we never doubt. It is a realization that we are not separate from God/Source – we are one and totally balanced in mind, body and soul.

You hold within your physical and mental structure 3 minds and 4 bodies. These consist of: the Conscious mind, the Subconscious and the Higher conscious mind. The conscious mind relates to logic and sends messages to the subconscious mind. The subconscious has no reasoning and believes everything the conscious mind is telling it. So you certainly need to re-educate the subconscious. Then you have the higher conscious mind; this is your connection to Source. The area where you are given answers to your questions, by connecting to your 'gut feeling'. Listen to these spiritual messages from your higher consciousness; it is God/Source communicating with you.

As I described earlier, you also have 4 bodies, these connect to the mental, emotional, physical and spiritual bodies.

Mental body relates to the energy surrounding your physical body, holding in the aura all the thoughts you have ever had in this incarnation and all your past lives.

Emotional body deals with feelings and desires, you need to bring this area into balance by transcending the lower-self desires and live only with spiritual desires. It will take time, but it can happen in this lifetime.

Physical body, this is a dense energy that you are born into. The idea is to resurrect this to a Light body – which can be attained through the Ascension process. [More on Ascension later.] The physical body is a vehicle that carries your soul around in this incarnation. When it is time for you to go home, the shell or physical body will be cast off and your soul will rise to the higher dimensions of reality, where you will continue to exist and grow.

Spiritual Body, your most beautiful body made of pure Light infused with the Christ Consciousness. This will be strengthened during your Ascension process.

All aspects of your consciousness need to be expanded and balanced during this lifetime; even more now than ever before. Everything that is happening on this planet is gaining momentum, speeding up. The closer you get to 2012/13 the more you will hear people saying 'There has got to be more to life than this' There is a change in consciousness going on with everyone. With all the pain and destruction still evident, people are sick and tired of it all.

It is down to every one of us to take responsibility for the healing of ourselves, and the planet. It is no good burying our heads in the sand and thinking that it has nothing to do with us. Everyone plays their part adding to the negativity, but most of the time we don't realise what we are doing. You need to recognise that every thought you have, everything you say and do will create a response. Cause and effect – as you give out negative vibrations, whether it is through anger, jealousy, hate etc. this creates a ripple effect within society with disastrous results. If you give out the positive vibrations through love, compassion, truth and kindness, this will also have an effect, but that will be of growth and spiritual understanding. So, yes, you can all make a positive difference to this planet with your thoughts, your actions and with love for your fellow man.

As you expand your consciousness through love, so you are presented with more spiritual gifts from the universe. This is the truth of your life here on this Earth.

Chapter Seven
Ascension, what does this mean?

How many times have you heard the word Ascension? What does it really mean?

It is a spiritual progression that will happen to every soul on this Earth at some time in their existence. The Ascension has never been in doubt; it is about the timing. It will happen when we reach a particular point in existence where we have released all negativity, and all fear based thinking; transcending the negative ego but raising our vibration to that of pure unconditional love and Light. It is a process by which our monad, soul and earthly personality become one.

We anchor the 'higher self' into the physical body in an integrated and balanced way. It is a realisation of our mission here on Earth, and seeing it through with love in our hearts and minds. It is dedicating our life to that of service to our fellow man and to Source/God. It is known as the 'I am Presence'

We have Ascension Angels that are here to help us through our individual Ascension process.

These Ascension Angels are guided with the power of Archangel Metatron – Chief of the Archangels. He is the creator of all the outer Light within the Universe.

We can call on him anytime to help us through our Ascension process.

This wonderful journey of enlightenment is a joy to

behold, it is not a chore, as it is working with love and the connections we all have to the 'Higher Beings' of Light and Love.

One of the questions I am often asked by clients or students is, 'How do I know my Ascension has begun?' My answer is this. From the moment we are born the Ascension process begins. We decided at soul level to be here at this Golden Age, or the Age of Aquarius, as it is known, as this is a time of rapid spiritual development.

All of the experiences whether good or bad, negative or positive will have an affect on our spiritual growth. We have to learn to release all of our fears such as prejudice, intolerance, hate, jealousy, envy, and greed, in fact all of the negative issues that have been part of our every day life for too long. This can only happen when we question ourselves, look within and start by being totally honest.

Ascension is living our life with love and compassion in our heart, showing kindness to our fellow man in our daily actions.

We will begin to recognise that we are more than the physical body; first we are spirit. We hold within our molecular structure the seed/atom of the Christ Consciousness, that is our natural essence. It is when we understand all of these concepts, and accept the truth of who we really are, that life becomes easier and more harmonious.

We can now stop living our life through illusion, and continue on our path of Ascension.

For more in-depth information read 'A New Light on Ascension' by Diana Cooper.

Chapter Eight
Reincarnation – Does it really happen?

I want to give you my understanding of reincarnation, not just my thoughts, but to share with you the experiences I have had, that have proved to me, without a doubt, that we do live many lives.

First let me ask you a question. Have you at sometime travelled to a place for the first time but it feels familiar to you, or have met someone for the first time but again feel you have seen them on another occasion, but cannot remember where or when? Yes, you possibly have been to this area before and met that person before but not in this lifetime. It is a connection at soul level, a remembering in the dark recesses of your mind, but a spark has been triggered and you are having recall of a past life. It may be just a flash of recognition but it is there.

Reincarnation is a complex subject to cover anytime, but I will try to explain in a simple way until it is time for you to have more in-depth understanding. There are many books on the subject and you just have to take what is presented to you with an open mind. You will know the truth when it is time to return home.

Let's be honest, doesn't it seem a waste of a life and experiences if we are only here once. What is gained by a one-off journey? How can we possibly right the wrongs that we have created in a lifetime? We need to journey back to meet up again with the people we had experiences with in a previous life. We may have unfinished business with that person. Coming back into another incarnation will allow us an opportunity to grow spiritually and to continue our learning process.

One question many people ask is, 'why can't we remember our past lives?' Nothing would be gained. We have to open our hearts and live our lives coming from kindness, love and compassion and it is only through living this way can we truly grow spiritually.

Each incarnation will allow us to progress and what we are ultimately aiming for is to become aware and recognise the seed or atom of the Christ consciousness that is within every human on this Earth. This will take many many years for us to attain this level of spiritual understanding, and acknowledging the part of us that is connected to God/Source. We are one; there is no separation.

Our soul has the knowledge of the Universe but wants to live many lives here on Earth to understand its connection to Source/God. Some people already feel in their heart that they have lived before; they are in no doubt about reincarnation. Sometimes it is just a 'knowing' inside that is so strong, you don't have to be told.

Through meditation, living and working with love, compassion and serving Source/God humanity will be given the key to unlock the stored memories within the soul. Allowing you access to the secrets of the Universe.

There are no rules about when we reincarnate again. We have about 200 incarnations here on Earth and some souls may come back immediately, although this is rare. Others may not arrive for 50 years or even more. The soul may decide to remain on the higher dimensions of reality to continue with its spiritual progression. It is all about the opportunities that are offered to us by the Spiritual Hierarchy.

We will sit with the Guides, Angels and all the relevant 'Beings' of Light and discuss where we will gain the knowledge that will help with our progression at soul level. We all have the potential to grow and the 'Higher Beings' will advise and guide us to the appropriate opportunities.

When we next journey here to Earth we will decide the country we will be born in, who our parents will be, the lifestyle we will have, whether we are to be rich, poor, disabled etc.

Many people cannot understand why we choose to come into a body that is disabled or in a situation where the child will be abused. It sounds abhorrent, but that is thinking in the old 3 dimensional ways. When you progress spiritually and understand the bigger picture you know that this is an opportunity to grow, it gives your soul a chance to rapidly build a beautiful connection with Source/God.

You may still ask, 'how do I know that reincarnation is true and that when we die we aren't just snuffed out of existence.' The time will come for you to have these answers and you will feel the truth inside of your heart.

I know the truth because I have had 2 out of body

experiences. More in-depth information is written in my first book. [Rahanni Celestial Healing – Embracing the Light.] I will give you a quick glimpse, as you may not have read my book.

Going back to 1981 my Mum had passed to spirit 2 years previous. I had great difficulty dealing with the grieving, but one day it hit me that Mum wasn't around anymore and I cried for 2 weeks. It was all the pent up emotion being released. As I continued with the tears, I was laying in bed and was aware that someone was standing at the side of me. It was my dear Mum. She took hold of my hand and before I could blink an eye I was out of my body and walking down a cobbled path with Mum. The feeling was unbelievable, just beautiful and there was so much love surrounding me. I will never be able to find the appropriate words to describe the love back home. [I feel this is where we really belong.] As I looked around there were flowers and colours that I have never seen on Earth. Little white houses similar to those in Greece were dotted about. As I continued to soak up the atmosphere and the beauty I glanced forward towards the end of the cobbled path and there in front of me was my beloved Dad, smiling in the way I remembered. He had passed to spirit when I was 2 years old. Oh, how I wanted to remain with them both. I didn't want to come back to the dark energy of the earth plane. But before I could say a word Mum spoke. 'Dad and I are together and very happy, so no more tears, I will take you back as you have so much to do. We will be waiting when it is your time to come home, but it is not yet.' I felt a jolt, I was back in my bed with tears streaming down my face, but they were tears of joy not sadness, for I knew in my heart that Mum and Dad were happy and well in their spirit life. They were both free of any previous pain they had suffered on Earth, so how could I possibly wish them back to the suffering that we endure here on this planet. I can now let them go with love in my heart, knowing we are still connected and they will continue to see my family grow.

This was my first experience of life after death. Yes we do move on to another realm of existence, but every human will go to the level that they have reached whilst being in human form. It is to do with the lessons we have learned and how much love we hold within our hearts.

There is more than one area for souls to return to. I have experienced just one, so it will remain to be seen where I will eventually go. I do know that my family will be waiting when I pass, but after a time of rehabilitation and connecting with loved ones we do eventually move on and progress, but this could take many years. Until we decide to reincarnate again and continue our fascinating journey through life on planet earth.

Chapter Nine
Karma – Law of Cause and Effect

How many times have you heard people say; 'what you give out you get back?' This relates to the deeds we have done in this life or previous lives. We create our reality with the thoughts we have, and the things we say and do. Everything on this Earth is vibrating with energy even our thoughts create a ripple affect within the universe. When something is said or done with intent, this will penetrate to where it was aimed and can create a reaction back to wherever the thoughts came from originally.

Let me give you an example. You are standing at the school gates waiting to pick up the children. As happens, groups of mums get together and talk. Maybe there is another mum standing on her own, not wishing to join the others, and for whatever reason this group of mums start talking about the individual lady, they are judging her and discussing her recent divorce, and of course everyone thinks they know all the reasons why this has happened and that has happened, they all seem to have a comment to make with regards to this lady and her situation. Oh, how groups of women love to pull people to pieces, it's unfortunate but it happens. This poor lady is unaware of what is going on, but she knows she has been feeling unwell of late. One reason could be the negative attacks on her from the group at the school.

As I explained earlier every word we speak has a vibration and if it is spoken with intent or venom the energy molecules will travel, in this instance, towards the divorced lady and will penetrate her aura. If this happens on a regular basis, the negativity will eventually enter her physical body and create imbalances within her system and she will feel unwell. But what many people tend to forget is what you give out you will get back. So the group of ladies had better take care, stopping and thinking before sending poison arrows to others, for they will return, of that you can be sure.

If on the other hand we send out positive vibrations of love and compassion and this is also sent with intent, it will be returned to us in a very positive way.

We can build a karmic situation of negativity or positive energy; it is all down to us and what we create with our thoughts and deeds.

Nobody gets away with anything, all is revealed when it is our time to pass over, or as I like to say – go home. Our guides and 'Higher Beings' of Light will take us through our entire life this time around, which is held in our Akashic Records or Book of Life. We are not judged, but are shown the outcome of all the situations we have created either negative or positive. This will help us decide and to understand the reason for coming back to Earth to right the wrongs. This is called personal karma. What we set in motion with the power of our conscious mind we are accountable for –always.

The second type is that of group karma. When we incarnate into this world we are born into groups based on skin colour, religious affiliations and so on. When a person is born into a black or Asian body, he or she will have to deal with prejudice at sometime, because of the different level of spiritual understanding of many souls on this planet. This person may take on the karmic lessons of that group.

We also have National karma. As we have seen many times over the years ego plays a big part in not just individual lives, but situations become a national problem. One country will feel more powerful than another, which has been shown with the wars that have taken place. Everyone becomes indoctrinated with egotistical ideas and values and will try to force their ways of thinking on others. Wanting power – to be in control.

In a way all karma could be called personal karma. Because at soul level before incarnation we decide which country we will be born into, the colour of our skin, who our families will be, whether we are rich or poor, good health or poor health. Our soul decides the lessons we need to learn. This is all designed to help us grow spiritually and to eventually ascend. It is beautifully done.

So remember, what we give out we will get back. If we give out pain and suffering to others this will return to us at sometime in our existence. It could be this lifetime or our next, but it will return. If on the other hand we give out love, compassion and kindness, this will also return, in this lifetime –10 fold.

We have a choice, just remember the karma that could be created, so stop and think before jumping in and having any regret.

CHAPTER TEN

Meditation – Why is it important?

I cannot begin to tell you how important regular meditation is to every person on a spiritual journey. I wanted to give more information so I connected to my guide Thomas during my next meditation. We communicated through telepathy, which is a wonderful way to feel close to any guide.

I began by asking the questions that had been put to me by my students and clients. I will share these answers with you now.

As I relaxed into the meditation, I felt Thomas draw close. His love touches my heart every time we connect. I began the question. Why is meditation so important? Thomas explained in his gentle way. 'Within the silence of meditation you can touch the heart of the 'Supreme Being' God/Source whatever you feel comfortable saying. It is a union of minds – the Divine mind of God/Source and the soul of the child of God/Source, you the personality on this earth plane. It is your recognition of the Divine spark held within your own mind and physical body whilst here on Earth, going through your experiences, your lessons. As you relax and draw in the breath of God/Source, this will help to raise your vibration to higher dimensions of reality. We in turn recognise what you are doing and we will lower our vibration to meet you halfway. By doing this on a regular basis it allows us to build a stronger bond or connection with you. It is also a much easier way of getting messages of importance to you. Aiding you on your journey. Do you understand?'

I thanked Thomas and said yes, this is also my understanding. I asked Thomas if he had any further information with regards to meditation. Yes, he had a reply.

'So many of you on Earth say you haven't got the time to meditate, your life is so busy. It's all very well being there for others, helping them with your healing, teaching and all the family issues, but what about you and your needs? Do you think so little of yourself that you cannot give 20 minutes of your time to help yourself and connect with the Father that gave you life. Can you not find the appreciation for all of the beauty that surrounds you? Unfortunately this is what happens, you are busy busy rushing around wearing yourself out to such a degree that you are not able to enjoy all the gifts that are offered to you from the universe, which is precisely what is presented to you in your meditative state.

May I give you more explanations of what happens during meditation on a regular basis?

You have chakras or energy centres that run through the centre of your physical body, they are connected to your nervous system. They are spiralling discs of Light and energy; this is what keeps you alive. As you begin to meditate on a regular basis these centres will glow with soft Light that will increase in size and brilliance as you continue your meditation. Their colours get brighter as they expand and this also helps to heal your physical body if it is out of balance.' Thomas continued, when he is on a roll there's no stopping him, but that's why I love our communications. Sorry, I digress! Thomas, it's back to you.

'It is so important to maintain a positive attitude and a feeling of love held in the heart centre. This is very good for your development, but saying that, do not force anything; it has to flow from your inner heart centre with love and compassion. There are so many excellent books to read with regards to meditation. I suggest you seek out the book that feels right for you.' I thanked Thomas for his words of wisdom and said I would pass this on to my students.

I would also like to add that through meditation it allows you to understand what is going on in your life and what is happening to you as a person. You see things in a different perspective. It is wonderful for releasing stress, but most important it is time for you.

As you relax your mind so the physical body will benefit. Your heart rate slows that in turn helps your circulation and the digestive system. So you can see the benefits already.

Meditation doesn't just have to be indoors in a quiet atmosphere, that is fine sometimes but to meditate outside in nature is pure bliss. All you need is to find an area where there are trees, so your back can rest on the tree. This is great because you will connect with its energy, you will feel the vibration the more you relax into it. Never force anything, just let it happen. Focus on your breathing in the solar plexus and if you have mundane thoughts appear in your mind, just recognise them and let them go. Don't judge yourself if it takes a while. It will happen the more you practice.

One suggestion, don't meditate after a heavy meal you will possibly fall asleep. Usually the best time is morning, but saying that I find around nine in the evening is good for me. It is up to the individual, try a few different times and see what suits you. If of course you are outdoors you can be more flexible.

Remember, you are not in trance, just a relaxed state of mind. Just enjoy the experience and who knows what might be presented to you.

Prayer = Speaking with God/Source.

Meditation = Listening to the answers.

CHAPTER ELEVEN
What is the 'Age of Aquarius'?

We hear mentioned many times the Age of Aquarius, so what is it? Let me explain about the 'Ages.' Every two thousand years or so, changes take place within the Universe. These changes do not only affect Earth but all planets within. It is an astrological era in which increased spirituality and harmony are said to characterize people's lives. So the Age of Aquarius is one of 12 astrological ages approximately 2000 years long. Many believe it is the beginning of a road towards enlightenment and expansion of consciousness. It is also known as the feminine era. We have had 2000 years of the masculine energy with the Age of Pisces. As these years progressed it was also a time of great change with regards to technology. If we look back over the past 20 years or so, we can see how everything is gaining momentum, moving faster. For instance take computers – 20 years ago they were so big and so slow in comparison to now, they are so tiny yet can store within their memory banks much knowledge and information, which reaches out to anyone anywhere in the blink of an eye. So everything changes, nothing stays the same; if it did we couldn't grow or progress.

The Age of Pisces being the masculine era needed strength, will and power and the use of the masculine mind promoting technology. In one respect this was required, but as with everything, it got out of control with all the wars, crime and negativity. Society had to change, or should I say humanity needed a change in consciousness, as this planet could not sustain another 2000 years of masculine vibrations. Hence we are now of the feminine energy, the age of love, compassion and truth. This is also balanced with wisdom, power and love.

The female is finding her inner strength and can now take back her power; she is in control of her life, no one else. Unfortunately the male species is in fear of this change and attitude within the woman. They feel they are losing the power and control that was theirs for the past 2000 years. But Universal Law is about balance. The Age of Aquarius is a wonderful time of discovery, finding out who we really are. If we are masculine or feminine at this time, it is a chance for us to balance both sides of our mind and body.

If we have been too much in our masculine side, showing anger, aggression and control, we can now open our heart centres and bring out the feminine side of love and compassion. If on the other hand we have been dominated by too much of the feminine energy, quiet and subservient, then it is the time to claim our inner strength and stand up for what we believe.

These changes won't happen over night, but this is the Golden opportunity for all of humanity to recognise the need for change and to do something about it, for the sake of every one of us on this planet and to help life to continue, but with love and compassion.

More emphasis will be put on growing organic foods, caring for the planet, the animals and using resources that have been available to us for many years, such as herbs, plants, healing, music and crystals. Plants will be grown with the aid of the new moon and full moon. Many gardeners are doing this already, growing vegetables within certain phases of the moon, and it has been very successful.

We are talking about our spiritual connections. More and more books are being written with all of these changes in mind. You can pick up a book on spiritual awareness in any good bookshop. Depending how far you are on your spiritual path you will be able to find the book or information which will help you grow. There are also active groups you can join for meditation, or spiritual enlightenment, a coming together of like-minds.

So much is offered to any of you searching to find your path or place in society, combined with spiritual understanding. Don't run before you walk, there is no rush. What you don't find on this journey you will find on your next incarnation.

Chapter Twelve
Understanding Soul Mates.

In the healing work that I do I will often hear clients say they don't understand why their relationship has broken up because they thought they had found their 'soul mate'. In other words they were expecting to be with their partner for the rest of this incarnation.

Because this hasn't happened they feel rejected, let down and feel all the hype about soul mates is a load of hogwash. This is not so, they have only one interpretation of the meaning of soul mate. I want to explain in a simple way how and why soul mates come into our lives.

A soul mate is not necessarily someone that will be with you for the rest of your life – yes, this does happen with some relationships, but it is rare. The majority of these soul mate connections are for different reasons. The person concerned may only stay in your life for about 5 years; they will reach a point in their life when they will know it is time to move on. The other person is distraught, but what they fail to realize is souls mates may only stay for a short while, because during their time together they will both learn many lessons from the relationship. It may well be that you have helped the other person to open their heart centre and they will begin to have a change in consciousness. You have helped them understand how releasing negativity and fear based thinking can give them a better quality of life. So nothing is wasted, everyone will gain from the time spent together. You on the other hand, although initially upset will at sometime realize that he or she wasn't the person that you thought they were. You begin to feel a sense of relief and know that it is time for you to move on. I am not saying this will be easy, but if you see things from a different perspective and not judge the other person, you will have gained so much from the relationship.

It is one of the problems being in a physical body and living a life here on earth, when it comes to relationships we have to have control, and we think that whatever we are feeling the other person should be feeling the same. This is very hard to explain, but no two people are ever the same. We are individuals with different thoughts and feelings, we have different needs at different times, and how we feel at the beginning of a relationship is not necessarily how we will feel 5 years on. Everything changes, nothing stays the same, if it did, we couldn't progress and move on.

Always remember, you decided at soul level that you would both be together in this incarnation, only at your higher level of understanding do you fully accept this.

We search for a reflection of our self; we search for perfect harmony, a love connection, and a joyous connection to a partner for the rest of this life. We only understand life from a perspective of the old 3 dimensional way of thinking and living. When you raise your vibration to a spiritual understanding you shift your consciousness to a higher level and know in your heart that love and compassion is your true essence. You will also know the benefit of a soul mate relationship. It is more than a sexual connection, it is a melding of hearts and minds, you become as one but with a different understanding and flexibility within the relationship. It is built on trust not fear, rejection or insecurities. When you are with your soul mate you understand not only the complexity of the union, but also the beauty of it.

Now this may not sit very comfortable with some as you read this, but you can have a soul mate relationship and a physical one with a partner of the same sex. No judgement is made at any time within the spiritual hierarchy. Your guides and Angels know you have free will, freedom of choice and they will also know that there was possibly unfinished business in a previous incarnation that will need to be resolved this time around.

You will find that a woman preferring a partner of the same sex will feel more comfortable with her own gender. There is sometimes a fear of getting to close to the male – it feels too dominating and controlling. So she will seek a relationship with a woman and will embrace the warmth, love and softer side of the female energy, as it is not so threatening.

The male/male relationship works on a similar principle; they will feel more comfortable within their own masculine group. The male may have a fear of the female energy. Maybe they had an overbearing Mother and have shied away from repeating the earlier uncomfortable years of their life. They feel more comfortable with the same sex relationship.

What we as humans fail to realize is that we are all

androgynous – perfectly balanced in masculine and feminine energies. The fact that we are drawn towards one sex than we are another is to do with the lack of balance within ourselves. It can be fear related or just the safer option.

Our soul mate may not necessarily be here on Earth, but in another dimension of reality. We will possibly meet up again when it is time to return home.

Just to close this chapter I wish to add, that as we continue to search outwardly for the passion, the part of us we feel is missing from our life, we are sure to fail, because what we desire is not outside of our self but inside. It is an inner 'knowing' of our connection to God/Source. The unconditional love we search for is always to be found within our own heart.

Chapter Thirteen
What happens when we die?

This is a very controversial subject and I will only be giving you my understanding from my perspective and how it has been shown to me by my guides and Angels.

Death will be a different experience for every human on this planet. When we pass to spirit the amount of spiritual understanding we have gained will decide the level of existence we will move to in the next realm.

So many people fear death, it is fear of the unknown. My clients and students put the same questions to me. 'Is death painful? where will I go? I don't want to leave my family.' I will try to alleviate your fears of death and believe me I had the same questions when I was younger, but through my experiences all has been revealed to me and I hold no more fear. I wish to share these experiences with you now.

First I will tell you that I have had two out of body experiences to date. One after my Mum passed to spirit and the other when I was attuned to Rahanni Celestial Healing on the 4th August 2002. [The story of this is in my first book –Rahanni Celestial Healing – Embracing the Light.] On both occasions I can honestly say the feeling of pure unconditional love surrounded my whole being. It is so difficult to explain because like most things they need to be experienced to be understood and appreciated. All I can do is speak of my individual experience and hope you can envisage what I am trying to relay.

I am also able to channel Ascended Masters, Archangels and Angels. In other words communicate with 'Higher Beings' of Light. If I have a question that needs an answer and I haven't actually had the experience I will contact one of my guides and they will try to explain in simplified terms by helping me to feel the emotion or the physical condition. I must say I feel very humble and privileged to have this communication with my guides. It is so beautiful. Sorry – I digress.

So when we are near the time for releasing our physical body and passing on to spirit what actually happens?

You at soul level are ready to move to a higher dimension of reality, ready to release all of the pain that goes with being in human form. You are surrounded by guides, Angels and members of your family who will draw close helping you to return home and guide you back to your natural essence, helping you also to understand that firstly you are spirit.

The atmosphere in the room changes as the beings of Light come closer. The room may become hazy with the build up of spiritual energy. The person about to depart this world will see a white light, so bright that you don't always realise you need to go to this light. So it is dimmed slightly to make it easier to see and you feel yourself surrounded by so much love as your soul ascends and leaves the physical body. As the soul rises up towards the next dimension you are greeted by a reality that is comfortable and familiar to you. It is a reality that you have created whilst being in a physical body on Earth.

So for instance, however you have lived your life

here on Earth this is what you will create on the spirit side of life. This is a reality that is familiar, so it doesn't seem as though too much has changed. But this is the most important point; if you wish to create a different life for yourself on the other side you can do so. Before this happens you will possibly go to an area for healing and rehabilitation, especially if you have suffered from a disease of some kind in your physical body on earth. Guides and Angels will surround you constantly helping to heal you at soul level.

As you progress you are given many opportunities to experience many new things, such as a chance to go to the Halls of Learning to find out more about – maybe gardening, music, art, healing. Whatever you feel you would like to have been able to do in your earthly life but somehow it always eluded you. You can do anything in the spirit world, especially if it will benefit your soul's growth.

You will reach a point of understanding that whenever you wish to travel or be in a beautiful garden you will know that this can be accomplished with just your thoughts.

Don't forget what I have said before, you create your reality with the thoughts you have. It is no different back home.

Life after death can bring new knowledge and wisdom for you in many ways, but you will be shown how every step of the way.

You still have a body in the spirit world but it is a Light body that is evolving as time progresses, the difference is, it is not heavy and dense like your old physical body. It radiates your natural essence of pure unconditional love and compassion.

Just one other point I wish to make, if you are sitting with a member of your family waiting for them to pass, don't be surprised if that person gives the impression that they have rallied round and you feel it is ok to leave for a while to go and have a cup of tea or maybe go home and try to get some sleep. But when you are not in the room they have slipped away, they have passed. They wanted to be alone or just with a nurse. You feel guilty, saying you should have stayed longer, but what you fail to understand is that they wanted it this way, they couldn't deal with all the fuss and they certainly didn't want you to see them take their last breath, because they know that's how you will remember them. They want you to remember seeing them at peace.

How many times do we hear people say 'It looked as though he/she had a smile on their face' Yes, exactly, they have returned to their natural home and it is a smile of love and recognition. So don't be sad, be happy that they have found inner peace and tranquillity.

When it is your time to go home, don't worry about leaving loved ones behind; you will be able to connect with them whenever you wish. They are but a touch away, but in another dimension of reality. As long as you hold them within your heart you will always be able to see them growing and living their lives. Your new life will be full of joy and freedom. You will see as I did the beautiful flowers and colours that will never be seen on this earth plane, you will sense love from every area of your new life. You will be free of pain, free from anger and all of the fears that we have had to deal with on Earth. So please do not fear death, when the time comes for us to return home, embrace it with love in your heart.

I am adding another aspect to death by helping many of you to understand about miscarriage and abortion. These are two very difficult subjects but I hope you will take something positive from these words.

When your soul decides to incarnate on to this earth plane; you will choose your parents, the country you will live in, if you are to be rich or poor, healthy or unhealthy. These are the experiences your soul needs to go through to help it grow spiritually. This is all decided at soul level. Being here on this earth is the quickest way for you to expand your consciousness.

You have a soul that is the closest part to God/Source; you also have a 'higher consciousness' that will connect with your physical mind and body. When a foetus is in the Mother's womb it has only the 'higher consciousness', the soul does not come into the baby until it is born, approximately 7 hours after. This 'higher consciousness' has telepathy and it knows everything the Mother is thinking and it also knows the experiences that she needs to go through. One of those experiences could be losing a baby either through miscarriage or abortion.

If the Mother decides it isn't the right time to have a child; the foetus will understand and knows that it will be aborted. No judgement is made at any time but the foetus will remove its 'higher consciousness' in preparation of the termination. It will take its energy back home and wait for the correct time to return.

Many women go through much pain and guilt after the event. I am here to tell you; please let the negative thoughts go. You have not been judged. The 'Higher Beings' of Light knew you had to go through this experience. They communicated with the foetus and helped it return home.

All I ask of you is to mentally connect with this little one and thank it for helping you to go through this experience and explain you will ask the baby to return when you are in a position to start a family. [If this is meant to be in this incarnation.] You can now let go of any guilt or pain that you may be feeling, and know in your heart that everything happens for a reason.

Living on this Earth is not just about experiencing all happy and delightful things; nothing is gained unless you experience the sad and painful. Everything in the universe is about balance, you can't have wet without dry, hot without cold, negative without positive. This is life.

How can you be of help to others if you haven't had the experiences? This is what makes you the special person you are. So from today I want you to know in your heart that you have done nothing wrong. You do not make mistakes; you have experiences. Learn from them.

Please understand this; what has been discussed here doesn't give anyone the right or easy option to act irresponsibly with regards to abortion; you still need to have respect for your body. This isn't a get out clause.

Chapter Fourteen

How to get the best out of life.

We have spoken about death and dying, now let us talk of life and living. I will just return to the earlier discussions in chapter nine about creating karma – what you give out so it will return from whence it came. We are talking about creating the reality you wish to live in. You have choices. You can live a happy, loving and joyful existence full of positive thoughts and energy or you can continue with a life of worry, anger, insecurities, fear and a negative mindset. It is up to you every time. We cannot blame others for what is happening in our life, you decide, no one else.

I hear so many clients blaming their spouse, partner or a member of their family for the difficult situation they are in at this present time. What they fail to grasp is that they have allowed this situation to happen. Let me give you an example; You are in a relationship, where at the beginning was exciting and everything you ever wanted. Now after 3 years or so the relationship has changed. The person you are living with is miserable, always moaning and has also become quite abusive, either verbally or physically. You cannot understand why this caring person you knew and loved has become a monster. You continue with the relationship, forgiving and hoping that this person you share your life with will eventually change. But as time goes on there is no change, in fact the situation has become intolerable. So why do you stay in this relationship? It evidently has run its course; you have tried everything to get it back on track, but to no avail. You are tired, angry and hurt. 'But I still love him,' that is the reply I always hear.

I find this very sad, as I know you cling on in the hope that in time the situation will return to how it was originally. In your heart you must know the truth of the relationship and how it is now, but you live in fear of living alone. The same words are spoken time after time. 'How will I cope?' So you stay in a relationship that is painful, without love and possibly dangerous. Why oh why do people continue to put themselves through such torture every day? They have so little confidence or self-esteem, all this has been taken from them over time, or should I say, they have allowed this to happen.

Clients will often ask; 'how can I deal with this? I couldn't leave because of the financial situation'. What everyone needs to recognise is, once again they have a choice, they can continue with the relationship as it is now, and goodness knows where it will end. Or you can start by saying, 'I am worth more than this, I do not deserve to be treated in this way and I deserve some respect'. This is about questioning yourself and who you think you really are. Yes, you do deserve better, but only you can make it happen.

Sometimes we need to go to counsellors or healers to initially give us the inner strength to deal in a positive way with our issues. When you feel the changes taking place within, then you know you can do something positive about getting your life back.

Always remember the choices you have. By staying you are stating that everything is fine, but choice number two is the better option. No, I am not prepared to continue to be manipulated and treated unfairly any longer; it's time to move on. I am not saying it will be easy, but anything that is worthwhile will need a lot of work. But it will pay dividends in the end. Financial situations will get sorted; there is so much help out there. CAB is wonderful for giving advice on many subjects and they have many contacts.

The fact that you have become stronger and are feeling more self worth will make all the difference. You will find that there are many people who have been through a similar situation and will be only to pleased to offer help and advice.

Don't underestimate the love that surrounds you and never forget all of the Archangels and Angels that are waiting for your call for help. As I have said before, not one of them can do anything unless you ask for the help; that is universal law. They cannot interfere, as they know you have free will.

So you can create the reality that you want, by the words you say, the thoughts you give out and the things that you do. Every thought you have is energy vibrating out into the universe or ether, so these thoughts will be created especially if they have a strong intent.

If you want a life of joy, health and love for your family and yourself, then create it with your mind. Put out what you want and **not** what you don't want. This is so important.

Situations can change over night simply by the thoughts that are released out into the universe. Now is the time to take control and have the life you deserve, for yourself and your family.

A wonderful book I will recommend is 'The Secret' by Rhonda Byrne. It gives so much insight of how to create a positive reality. Do read this, I am sure you will benefit.

Chapter Fifteen

A simple approach to life.

I want to begin this chapter with a quote from White Eagle's teachings. This is a beautiful way to understand how to live harmoniously.

> There is always something beyond
> all earthly things
> Something elusive which cannot be
> caught, trapped and harnessed
> by the human mind
> It is so free, so subtle, that it can only
> be realised in your own heart.

When you understand the meaning of this you are on a spiritual path. All I can say, for any of you that wish to connect with a Spiritual Teacher, then please read White Eagle's books. They are so profound and a joy to read. He touches your heart with so much love held in every sentence.

This brings me to another example of the hierarchy getting a message across. Going back years to my earlier connection to Angels, I was having a difficult time trying to channel spiritual knowledge. I began to feel frustrated so I put everything to one-side for a while. It was coming up towards Christmas and the family were gathered together around the table when one of my Granddaughters asked me to pull a cracker with her. When unusually I managed to get the bigger end of the cracker with the gift inside.

As I pulled hard, there was the loud crack! And thrown into my lap was a key ring, nothing unusual with that except attached to it was a hanging foam cutout saying 'Trust.' My Granddaughter laughed and said 'Grandma, I think this one is definitely for you.' I somehow felt she was right. I still have that key ring and if ever any doubt creeps into my mind, [not often, I hasten to add.] I open my desk drawer and there it is, reminding me, 'Trust' This isn't coincidence, it is called synchronicity. Explained as:' The experiences of meaningful alignments of events that seem to reveal a connection within the chaos to a higher order of being and a Divine Plan' [Wow! Definitely not my words.]

To be in synchronicity is to always be in the right place at the right time, to be in the flow of the Divine Plan, being in perfect harmony with everything. [Taken from the books of Dr. Joshua D Stone.]

So let us look at how we can simplify our lives, and to bring in more joy, love and abundance.

First we need to open our hearts to love and compassion. As I have stated many times before, what you give out so you will get back. If you want a life of love and joy, this is how you need to relate to others. We are here on this Earth to go through experiences, not all will be happy, some will be sad or painful, but we can learn from them. We do not make mistakes, we have experiences; this is the best way to understand why we go through so much in our lifetime.

I stated earlier in this book that we decided at soul level to be here at this time, going through many experiences, some happy some sad, but because of all this, we will grow spiritually. It most certainly is a journey of discovery and of understanding, finding out who we really are and recognising our connection to God/ Source.

We need to remember, there is no separation, we are from one Divine energy source, whether it be the trees, the plants, animals etc. There is no difference; of that we can be sure.

When you are out walking, how many times do you stop and look at what is around you? You notice trees, flowers, birds and animals, but do you really see the quality of life and feel the connection to God/Source and your self; probably not. We are so tied up with all our earthly pursuits, that these questions seem irrelevant and they go unanswered, or we just take them for granted. It is time now to look and see, touch and feel, listen and hear. Don't just accept all that surrounds you as being just 'there' feel things in your heart, touch the soil, the trees, the flowers and see them as never before. Their energy is a part of your energy. They are vibrating with Divine Light; this is what is keeping them alive and you.

Everyone is in such a hurry these days, and wants too much of the materialistic things in life. They push themselves beyond the limit at times creating ill health, worries and fears. Do try to look at life from a different perspective and appreciate all that has been offered to you on this beautiful planet. Appreciate the little things in life; they are worth so much more than you think.

Begin by getting into harmony with the natural forces of nature. Hug a tree – I know you feel like laughing, but have you ever tried? Go on, hug a tree, close your eyes and listen. You may start to feel a vibration around your body; you may feel a little light-headed. Good, that is you communicating with the vibration that is rippling throughout the universe. You are a part of this wonderful pulsing love which is available for all who are prepared to listen. The trees give us life, but we take that for granted. Trees need us as much as we need them. As we breathe out carbon dioxide, the tree uses this for its metabolism; therefore as they grow they give off oxygen, allowing us to breathe.

As I am writing this I am hearing the sound of Om! vibrating around my head. This is the primordial sound of creation. It really touches my heart and lifts my spirit. I just wanted to share that with you.

There are plenty of people ready to ridicule the spirit world. These people live in a world of darkness and do not yet understand about life and love. I am not making judgements at all, I just feel sad for those who have yet to connect with this reality of being, but I wish them well on their journey of discovery. All we can do is send love and light to these souls in the hope that soon they will have a change in consciousness and remember who they really are. Many people are beginning to open their hearts and it will happen to everyone at sometime in their existence.

You may ask, why do we need to recognise our spiritual connection, what can be gained?
I will tell you how your life will change beyond recognition. You will feel an inner peace and joy that

you have never known before. As your hearts open to its natural essence of love and compassion, you feel complete, a sense of belonging. You release fear and all negative ways of thinking. Don't take my word for it – become a part of all that is; the connection to your soul, the real you. For you have within, deep inside of your 'being' a seed/atom, the Christ Consciousness, your connection to the higher realms of Light and Love. I don't want to get too heavy here, but I always wish to share what I hold inside of my heart, sharing the love with you all.

When you first connect or become aware of your spiritual side, you will require patience. Now this hasn't been a virtue of mine or should I say, it wasn't earlier on at the start of my spiritual connections. We as humans are always in such a hurry – slow down and smell the roses. Enjoy the little things in life; accept that all will be revealed to you spiritually when the time is right. Your guides will know exactly when this is to be. They know your life-plan, so they will not rush you.

When you are in a quiet time, relaxing and unhurried, this gives the guides and Angels the perfect time to draw closer. They cannot enter a noisy, muddled mind. They will wait until you become aware of what is required for their connection.

Something I wish to convey to you is the importance of a healthy body. This can only be accomplished with a healthy mind. As you know, the body is a reflection of the mind. Continuing to have negative thoughts and worries only brings darkness into your aura which will eventually penetrate your physical body creating illness. I must mention diet and nutrition and how important this is for your spiritual growth.

I know you are probably saying, 'Oh here we go again, I have got to become a vegetarian.' No, I am not saying that, but what I want to point out is, if you continue to eat the heavy dense food that you have been used to it will take its toll and cause the bloodstream to thicken, adding to old age. You need to purify your body or the physical atoms, and to do this you need to eat pure food. If you continue to eat meat [your choice] this can transmit fears and vibrations that have been held in the minds of the animals before they were slaughtered, to feed you. Animals are a part of us; remember the universal energy that keeps them alive is also the life force you are derived from. There is no separation. So, putting it bluntly, as you consume the flesh of animals it is no different to eating your brother or sister. I know this sounds harsh, but think about it. But saying that,I do not want to brainwash you into doing something you are not yet ready for. But it is food for thought; excuse the pun.

This now brings me to water. So many therapists insist you drink 6/8 glasses every day. Now this may be fine for some people but not for everyone. I certainly cannot drink that amount. Too much can be a negative as you can reduce the amount of electrolytes in the body which has a detrimental affect on the liver and other organs. So be careful, go by your gut feeling about the appropriate amount for each individual. Filtered water if possible as town water has impurities and minerals that can harm the body. This sounds a bit doom and gloomy, but just stop and think, your body is precious, treat it with respect.

I want to discuss Chakras, so what are they and what is their purpose? Chakras are spiralling discs of energy. Think of a Catherine wheel as it spins, sending out colours and rays of light. We have 7 main chakras aligned with our spine, connecting to the nervous system. They spin out from the body creating the life-force keeping us alive. When we become unwell it shows in our aura, it becomes dim. The colours that should be radiating would be Red, Orange, Yellow, Green/Pink, Blue, Indigo and Violet/White. When a person is sick of mind or body these colours will change. They become muddy, grey or tinged in brown. Therefore creating within you a feeling of being tired, run down, lethargic or depressed. You begin to lose interest in all aspects of your life as you are utterly depleted.

If this is you, then take yourself off to a healer. They can balance your chakras and bring them back into alignment. There's no excuse as many therapists are available, if only you seek the help.

Start by taking responsibility for yourself and your well-being. Play some beautiful music – how many times do you do this and feel uplifted. It's all to do with vibration. The sound of the music resonates with our pineal gland at the back of our head, creating seratonin, the good feel factor. It doesn't matter what you are listening to; Tchaikovsky or Elvis, as long as it is creating a pleasant sound for your ears and relaxes you. [I wouldn't recommend heavy metal music; this can have a negative affect.]

This has been a chapter on the simple approach to

life, recognising how you can help yourself and have a better quality of life. No complications, just a simple truth.

Chapter Sixteen

Between two worlds.

I want to conclude this small book by giving you an insight to the understanding of the spirit world as I know it and see it. My truths are not necessarily your truths – all I can do is offer some food for thought, and maybe something of what I say will resonate with you and help as you move forward on your spiritual journey.

The many spiritual experiences I have had have brought great joy and love into my life. I wanted to share this with you and I hope I have been able to open your heart and mind to your own spiritual truth, and show you ways of bringing Light into your life.

The spirit world is but a touch away although in another dimension of reality – lighter and finer than that of the dense physical dimension of Earth.

Unless you are on a spiritual path it could be quite difficult for you to see with your physical eyes the beauty of the spirit world. A world of immense joy, love, compassion and beauty; some might call it heaven. It is a dimension where Angels, Archangels and all 'Higher Beings of Light exist. We are not separate from these wonderful 'beings' we are closer than we think. Before we incarnate on this Earth into physical form, we are surrounded by guides and Angels who teach and advise us with regards to our next incarnation. We have a Guardian Angel that has been with us in many incarnations and they will also progress with their spiritual growth; for they are here to serve humanity.

All it takes from us is trust and recognition of these guides. Just know that you are never alone – even in your darkest hour. You will always have at your side this beautiful 'being' of Light, giving help and support, all you are required to do is ask.

As the spiritual awareness grows on this earth plane the veil between the worlds will become finer, therefore making it easier to see and communicate with the other side of life, and with other dimensions of reality. For this to happen you need to expand your awareness, this will help you to gain access to the spiritual knowledge and wisdom that is held within the higher realms. There is so much more, but I am not going into great detail here, as I do not want to take you out of your comfort zone of understanding. There are so many books available that can do this justice, and remembering what this book is about – simplicity, no complications. I am just touching on the subject and trying to answer some of the questions which have been asked by clients and students; the simple version.

If the desire is to help yourself become a more caring and compassionate person by helping others to heal; the information here will help you to realize a dream of connecting to guides and Angels on a daily basis. Providing you work from the heart centre at all times. There is no room for ego on a spiritual path. This comes from the dark side of life not the Light. It takes many incarnations and experiences to become aware of who you really are. A soul in a physical body going through many of life's experiences; helping you to grow within your spiritual understanding.

As you become more aware of how to communicate with spirit you naturally feel your need for more information. This can be found by attending classes in your area, being with groups of like-minded people, as group work enhances the vibration. This allows you to become a channel to guides and 'Higher Beings' of Light and Love.

There are many books available on channelling and one I would certainly recommend is 'Opening to Channel' by Sanaya Roman. A book beautifully written and easy to understand.

Just returning to the spirit world and finding out what it's really like; I explained in my previous book [Rahanni Celestial Healing – Embracing the Light.] how I have had out of body experiences where I have been given the opportunity to connect with those on the other side of life. I have seen and felt the love and the beauty that surrounds everything and every 'being'. In the spirit world there is no separation, everything is one; from one Divine energy. We all have the ability to connect with these worlds of Light; we just need to be shown how.

Sometimes we will go to a medium to hopefully get a message from our departed ones. This is fine in one respect, but creates a problem in another. If we cannot let the person go and move on, this is creating ongoing pain for us. This is also hard for the departed one to move on, as they are held back with our sadness, we are not allowing them to move deeper into the Light. They need to go through experiences on the other side, but cannot progress until we release them within our heart. We do not stop loving them; we are accepting it is time to let them move on, as we need to do the same.

It is rather selfish for us to cling on, but when we are grieving the spiritual understanding of it all just gets pushed to the back of our minds. It is understandable. Do try to release them to the Light and let them return home peacefully. We will at the correct time meet with them again; then it will be our turn to go home.

All they want is for you to have a happy, loving and healthy life on Earth. If we are sad, they will be sad. If we try to remain positive and begin to bring some joy into our lives again, that will help them on their journey.

The many guides and Angels will care for them on their journey back home. Our family members that have now left us will meet up with departed Mums, Dads, children and animals who had left previously. They will spend much time together until they realize they need to progress in the spirit world. They will be given the opportunity to try many different areas such as going to the Halls of Learning where they will be presented with the option of becoming a musician or an artist, if this is what they were inspired to do but never really had the time on Earth. When we are in spirit we are eventually shown how to move from place to place just by our thoughts. So if you have wanted to travel, but was scared of flying, you don't have to worry now, just beam yourself there. It sounds a lot like 'Star Trek', but it's not far from the truth.

In time of course our guides will show us how to raise our vibration whilst on the other side of life. And when it is time for us to return to Earth in another incarnation we will be helped to make the decision that will affect our spiritual growth. We may have reached a point already that we do not need to return to Earth to continue evolving at soul level. We could be told it is our choice to either come back or remain on the other side and continue to teach new souls with their spiritual growth.

Oh! I can't begin to tell you how beautiful it is back home. Little white houses dotted about in a lovely countryside, with flowers and colour that will never be seen on this earth plane. Rivers, streams and waterfalls of pink and turquoise; mountains of violet and purple, giving off healing rays of Light. But it is the love you cannot deny, it stays with you forever. Even when you have only visited for a short while as I have, you never forget the quality of life and love; it stays in your heart always.

I just want to mention the Akashic Records or the Book of Life. This is to do with the karma we have created on earth; remember, cause and effect, what you give out will be returned at some time in our existence. Everything that we go through is noted. How we deal with the experience or situation. What we have created with our thoughts and actions will make a difference to our next incarnation. When we arrive home, we are shown the history of our life and the things we have done or said, and how it had affected someone else's life. We are creating our next journey and the experiences we still need to go through. If we gave out pain and suffering then believe me we will have to go through the same or similar experience in our next incarnation. We will also be given the feeling that we inflicted on others, the pain, the fear or trauma. We are given the emotion, not a pleasant experience I am sure, but what you give out etc. If on the other hand we offered love and compassion in this incarnation, we also have that returned, but 10 fold in this lifetime. We do not get away with anything. It is written in the Book of Life, the Akashic Records.

Chapter Seventeen
Healing Hands.

When you become aware of your spiritual self you will also understand how healing takes place, either for yourself or others. There is no mystery or secret with regards to healing. Everyone on this Earth has the ability to heal. Many are unaware and need to be shown how to connect to the healing rays of Light and how best to work with them.

Spiritual Healing – for this is where it originates, from the spiritual realms. It comes in many guises, but it matters not what title you place on this healing, either Rahanni, Reiki, Spiritual, Angelic, or Celestial. It all arrives and is channelled from God/Source. The Universal Life-Force, our natural essence. It is out there in abundance just waiting to be tapped into. It is a wonderful way of bringing balance back to the sick mind, body and soul. Saying all that, there will be times when conventional methods of healing will be required, such as antibiotics. Spiritual healing is not instead of; it is a complementary therapy working alongside conventional medicine.

Many problems arise within people's bodies because of the lack of spiritual awareness. We create a vast amount of our own problems simply by the thoughts we have. Anger, prejudice, resentment, insecurity. These are all fear-based ways of thinking and they come from the dark side of life not the Light. So to help with healing our self we need to overcome our fears and phobias and begin to think in a positive spiritual way.

You never force healing on anyone; they will eventually come of their own free will. Yes, you can offer to send distant healing to anyone anywhere in the world, for as you do it is always for the highest good of the person. You do not have any control over the outcome, in fact detachment is very important when healing. You have to understand you are just a channel for the healing Light to flow through. It is not down to us who gets better and who does not. It all relates to karma and why we have to go through many experiences. You have to learn from every situation and no matter how much healing is given, if the problem is karmic, it will not be changed. All healers must remember this.

When healing takes place you focus on the person being healed at soul level, this is paramount with healing. This way it helps the person to progress spiritually.

I wish to explain a little more in detail about the physical body and how it relates to our soul and aura. Our physical body is just a vehicle to carry the soul around on its journey in this incarnation. The soul is on a very high vibration of spiritual understanding, but the energy of this earth is too dense for the soul to remain without a vehicle – the physical body. The soul will arrive into our body approximately 7 hours after birth. It already has a higher consciousness that will be able to communicate with the Mother whilst in the womb. Entering this earth plane through the process of birthing, this little one knows of love, compassion and joy for this has been its home for quite sometime.

As the soul connects to the physical body it creates an energy field known as the aura. This aura keeps us alive and is created by the vibration of chakras [This was explained in an earlier chapter.] We can anchor many more than the original 7 main chakras, it is really down to our spiritual growth.

When we become unwell these chakras become out of balance. They lose their glow and radiance and if we have evolved to a higher level we will be able to see people's auras. The colours are dim, with tinges of brown or grey. This is the negative energy that needs to be cleared and healed. This is the time to seek out a healer to bring back our natural essence of Light into the body. We also have meridians flowing within the body; these will require attention also. This healing will do.

When a Practitioner commences the healing, he/she will not be working alone. Healing Light will surround both the client and healer. Light that is channelled through with the help of Archangels, Angels and many 'Higher Beings' of Light. Together we are trying to restore the balance of the mind, body and soul, bringing everything back into alignment for the highest good of the client. Every healing that takes place is for the highest good; there is no room for ego as I have said before. So when you channel the Light of God/Source you will be working from the heart centre with love and compassion and with intent.

It is so important that the Practitioner keeps him/herself in good health, living healthily, eating pure food and water and does not block the system with negative vibrations such a smoke. Remember to teach by example. Take time out for your self and recharge your batteries, so to speak. This can be done very easily by taking time out in nature or by the sea. The vibrations flowing from nature will enhance your aura as you breathe in deeply. Relaxation is also an important part for the therapist. The more effort we put in to becoming a pure channel the more sensitive we become to the life force surrounding all life.

It is very important to protect our self from negative and outside influences. This is done by visualising our aura wrapping itself around our body like an old Victorian cloak and seeing our self in a Golden bubble of Light. This will protect us from harmful and negative rays or vibrations. This we must do if we are to become involved with healing at any level.

Anyone can become a healer or a Light Worker, all we need is love, compassion and to be connected to the heart centre for the highest good of humanity.

Closing Comments.

I sincerely hope this book has given the 'newcomer' to spirituality a simple and basic understanding. Of course more details could be presented but that defeats the object of this book. It is basic spiritual knowledge. When you feel ready to move on and expand your understanding there will be plenty of other books to choose from, that will take you to the next level of your spiritual growth.

All I have tried to do is open your awareness and hopefully planted the seed of your understanding of why you are here. This 21st century is a wonderful time of exploration with regards to spirituality. Many experiences are offered to you all. So much you already know within yourself. Your soul has many answers, just find the way to retrieve them; meditation is a great help. Try connecting with like-minded people, as you will be able to share many spiritual experiences together.

I will leave you with a beautiful thought from White Eagle:

Say little
Love much
Give all
Judge no one
Aspire to all that is pure and good
and keep on – keeping on.

My blessings to you
I am Carol Anne Stacey
Founder/Teacher/Healer/Writer of Rahanni Celestial Healing.
www.rahannicelestialhealing.co.uk
Email: caraleigh@live.com